An Agenda for Improved Evaluation of Supercomputer Performance

A Report Prepared by the

Committee on Supercomputer Performance and Development
Energy Engineering Board
Commission on Engineering and Technical Systems
National Research Council

NATIONAL ACADEMY PRESS
Washington, D.C.   1986

NOTICE: The project that is the subject of this report was approved by the Governing Board of the National Research Council, whose members are drawn from the councils of the National Academy of Sciences, the National Academy of Engineering, and the Institute of Medicine. The members of the committee responsible for the report were chosen for their special competences and with regard for appropriate balance.

This report has been reviewed by a group other than the authors according to procedures approved by a Report Review Committee consisting of members of the National Academy of Sciences, the National Academy of Engineering, and the Institute of Medicine.

The National Research Council was established by the National Academy of Sciences in 1916 to associate the broad community of science and technology with the Academy's purposes of furthering knowledge and of advising the federal government. The Council operates in accordance with general policies determined by the Academy under the authority of its congressional charter of 1863, which establishes the Academy as a private, nonprofit, self-governing membership corporation. The Council has become the principal operating agency of both the National Academy of Sciences and the National Academy of Engineering in the conduct of their services to the government, the public, and the scientific and engineering communities. It is administered jointly by both Academies and the Institute of Medicine. The National Academy of Engineering and the Institute of Medicine were established in 1964 and 1970, respectively, under the charter of the National Academy of Sciences.

This is a report of work supported by Grant No. DE-FG05-85ER25008, from the U.S. Department of Energy, and Grant No. N00014-85-G-0233, from the Office of Naval Research, U.S. Department of the Navy, to the National Academy of Sciences.

Copies available from:

Energy Engineering Board
Commission on Engineering and Technical Systems
National Research Council
2101 Constitution Avenue, N.W.
Washington, D.C. 20418

Printed in the United States of America

Second Printing

COMMITTEE ON SUPERCOMPUTER PERFORMANCE AND DEVELOPMENT

E. F. INFANTE (Chairman), University of Minnesota
CLIFFORD N. ARNOLD, ETA Systems, Incorporated, St. Paul, Minnesota
ROBERT R. BORCHERS, Lawrence Livermore National Laboratory, Livermore, California
JAMES C. BROWNE, Department of Physics and Computer Science, University of Texas at Austin
BILL L. BUZBEE, Los Alamos National Laboratory, Los Alamos, New Mexico
ROBERT H. EWALD, Cray Research, Incorporated, Minneapolis, Minnesota
SIDNEY FERNBACH, Alamo, California
DUNCAN H. LAWRIE, Department of Computer Science, University of Illinois, Urbana, Illinois
JOANNE L. MARTIN, International Business Machines Corporation, Yorktown Heights, New York
VICTOR L. PETERSON, National Aeronautics and Space Administration, Moffett Field, California
PAUL SCHNECK, Supercomputing Research Center, Lanham, Maryland
JACK WORLTON, Los Alamos, New Mexico

Liaison with Energy Engineering Board

THELMA ESTRIN, School of Engineering and Applied Science, University of California at Los Angeles

Staff

DENNIS F. MILLER, Executive Director, Energy Engineering Board
JOHN M. RICHARDSON, Study Director, Committee on Supercomputer Performance and Development
ROBERT COHEN, Senior Staff Officer, Committee on Supercomputer Performance and Development
HELEN D. JOHNSON, Staff Associate, Energy Engineering Board
CARLITA M. PERRY, Administrative Secretary, Committee on Supercomputer Performance and Development

ENERGY ENGINEERING BOARD

*HERBERT H. WOODSON, (Chairman), The University of Texas at Austin
WILLIAM R. GOULD, (Chairman), Southern California Edison Company, Rosemead, California
ALLAN J. BARD, The University of Texas at Austin
*ROBERT J. BUDNITZ, Future Resources Associates, Inc., Berkeley, California
THELMA ESTRIN, University of California at Los Angeles
CHARLES F. GAY, Arco Solar, Chatsworth, California
S. WILLIAM GOUSE, Mitre Corporation, McLean, Virginia
NICHOLAS J. GRANT, Massachusetts Institute of Technology, Cambridge
*BRUCE H. HANNON, University of Illinois at Urbana-Champaign, Urbana
GARY H. HEICHEL, University of Minnesota, St. Paul
JOSEPH M. HENDRIE, Brookhaven National Laboratory, Upton, New York
WILLIAM W. HOGAN, Harvard University, Cambridge, Massachusetts
BAINE P. KERR, Pennzoil Company, Houston, Texas
HENRY R. LINDEN, Gas Research Institute, Chicago, Illinois
EDWARD A. MASON, Amoco Research Center, Naperville, Illinois
ALAN D. PASTERNAK, Energy Consultant, Sacramento, California
THOMAS H. PIGFORD, University of California, Berkeley
ADEL F. SAROFIM, Massachusetts Institute of Technology, Cambridge
MAXINE L. SAVITZ, The Garrett Corporation, Los Angeles, California
WESTON M. STACEY, JR., Georgia Institute of Technology, Atlanta
RICHARD STEIN, The Stein Partnership, New York, New York
THOMAS E. STELSON, Georgia Institute of Technology, Atlanta
LEON STOCK, University of Chicago, Illinois
GEORGE S. TOLLEY, University of Chicago, Illinois
DAVID C. WHITE, Massachusetts Institute of Technology, Cambridge
RICHARD WILSON, Harvard University, Cambridge, Massachusetts

Technical Advisory Panel

HAROLD M. AGNEW, GA Technologies, Inc., Solana Beach, California
FLOYD L. CULLER, JR., Electric Power Research Institute, Palo Alto, California
CHAUNCEY STARR, Electric Power Research Institute, Palo Alto, California
ALBERT R.C. WESTWOOD, Martin Marietta Labs, Martin Marietta Corporation, Baltimore, Maryland

Staff

Dennis F. Miller, Executive Director, Energy Engineering Board
Helen D. Johnson, Staff Associate
Cheryl A. Winter, Staff Assistant

---

*Term expired June 30, 1986

PREFACE

This report presents the results of a brief study to assess current methods of evaluating supercomputer performance, identify opportunities for improvement, and recommend the outlines of a research agenda to realize these opportunities.

A substantial scientific community and body of literature are devoted to computer performance measurement and evaluation. Impressive successes have been achieved in theory, prediction, and experimentation for systems that have sequential architecture and applications that involve data handling and manipulation. Less successful and mature are the methods and measurements for evaluation of system performance when scientific problems are run on supercomputers of diverse architectural characteristics. Performance evaluation is especially important for supercomputers, not merely because they are a costly resource but, more fundamentally, because they must often work at the limits of their performance to produce the results wanted. The complexity of these systems, together with the increasing diversity of computing architectures becoming available, makes evaluation of supercomputer performance more problematical, yet more important, than for the more common midrange computer systems. Moreover, what is learned about the performance of operational systems can be expected to guide the design of future systems.

The U.S. Department of Energy and the Office of Naval Research, in response to these needs, arranged with the National Research Council to assess the improvements attainable in performance evaluation of large-scale scientific computers.

On the basis of its own experience and its contacts with members of the research and development community, the committee established for the purpose concluded that current performance measures and methods for supercomputer evaluation do indeed need significant improvement. Moreover, the committee judged that no well developed scientific foundation exists for supercomputer performance evaluation.

In consequence, this report paints in broad strokes the outlines of this topic, its problems, and its possibilities. Filling in the details of the panorama requires the successful accomplishment of research outlined in this report. In addition, it requires the help of a formal mechanism of the research community to track, assess, and disseminate research results with a view to bringing about commonly accepted methodologies of performance evaluation.

The report is directed to persons in the federal agencies and elsewhere who fund research, and to the industrial and academic researchers who perform it.

On behalf of the committee members I wish to voice our gratitude for the interest and support of Donald M. Austin, of the U.S. Department of Energy, and Charles J. Holland, of the Office of Naval Research. Carl Diem, of Cray Research; Troy L. Wilson, of International Business Machines Corporation; and the members of the Parallel Processing Group of the National Bureau of Standards generously shared their knowledge with members of the committee. In the course of his review of the report manuscript, Peter J. Denning, of the Research Institute for Advanced Computer Science, provided the committee with valuable contributions to the topics presented here. The task was initiated by Dennis F. Miller, Executive Director of the Energy Engineering Board. The contributions to the committee's work by John M. Richardson and Robert Cohen, of the board's staff, are most gratefully acknowledged. Carlita M. Perry handled the manifold administrative tasks with grace, tact, and competence.

Finally, I wish to thank the members of the committee for their extensive contributions of time and effort, and for their selfless sharing of knowledge and experience.

I acknowledge all these contributions with sincere gratitude.

                                              E. F. Infante, Chairman
                                              Committee on Supercomputer
                                                  Performance and Development

CONTENTS

SUMMARY... 1

1 INTRODUCTION... 9

   The Problem / 9
   Approach to the Study / 11

2 PRINCIPLES FOR THE EVALUATION OF SUPERCOMPUTERS.......... 13

   The Context for Evaluation / 13
   Criteria for Evaluation / 14
   Matching Computational and Application Characteristics / 17
   The Cycle of Performance Evaluation / 17

3 THE CURRENT STATE OF THE ART IN EVALUATION OF SUPERCOMPUTERS.. 21

   Lessons from the Past / 21
   Performance Metrics / 23
   Test Programs for Performance Measurement / 24
   Analytical Approach to Performance Evaluation / 27
   Summary / 28
   References / 29

4 IMPROVEMENTS ATTAINABLE IN PERFORMANCE EVALUATION........ 31

   Models and Classification Schemes / 32
   Requirements for Producing Measurements / 37
   Five Stages in Performance Evaluation / 38
   System Performance Issues / 41
   Conclusion / 42
   References / 43

5 AN AGENDA FOR RESEARCH..................................... 5.1

    Opportunities / 5.1
    Research Program Specifications / 5.2
    Conduct of Research Program / 5.7

APPENDIX A STATEMENT OF TASK.................................... 53

APPENDIX B ANNOTATED SHORT BIBLIOGRAPHY OF ALGORITHM- OR........ 55
    APPLICATION-SPECIALIZED COMPUTER SYSTEMS

SUMMARY

During the past ten years a substantial literature on methods for the evaluation of the performance of computer systems was developed by the community of industrial and academic scientists and engineers. Noteworthy successes were achieved in the evaluation of performance of sequential architecture machines on applications comprising data reduction and manipulation. For such systems and applications, theoretical models and performance measures were developed with good predictive power. In essence, these models enjoy a sound scientific underpinning. Much less success and maturity, however, characterize the methods and measures of performance evaluation of computer systems that must execute scientific applications whose widely varied computational structures lead to diverse and poorly characterizable workloads.

Performance evaluation is especially difficult and problematical for supercomputers--general purpose systems devoted to large-scale scientific computations--because of their complexity, diversity of architectures, and the demanding nature of the applications they undertake. The qualitative nature of the performance evaluation for supercomputers departs from an emphasis on throughput and balanced maximal utilization of all components of the system. The new emphasis is primarily on the computational speed of the processor(s) and secondarily on assuring that specific demands by the computational structure of the application on a particular component of the system do not impede the potential performance of the whole system.

Thus, in spite of progress, methods and measures for the evaluation of supercomputer performance need further improvement. Metrics, such as millions of floating point operations per second (MFLOPS) and millions of instructions per second (MIPS), and certain test program benchmarks are repeatedly used. However, the interpretation of these quantities and their use can be contradictory and misleading. There is, at this time, no commonly accepted methodology for the evaluation of the performance of supercomputer systems and no standard set of metrics for the representation of performance. More powerful evaluation methods are essential for comparing competing systems, allocating available machine resources, matching specific computing tasks to specific hardware, and designing new systems. To be useful, evaluation methods should encompass the complexity of supercomputer systems, their variety, and their diverse applications. These are complex and novel expectations of the evaluation process. Progress is being made, but there are strong indications from the current debate in the literature and technical journals, as well as in the trade press, that performance evaluation of supercomputer systems has not developed to the desired level of sophistication and coherence.

The importance of performance evaluation grows as the capability and cost of the system grow. Supercomputers, vital components in the industry and defense of the nation, are used precisely because they provide the highest performance; and they are acquired at high cost. Use of the full capability of such resources is an obvious aim.

The evaluation of a supercomputer should be based on more than its speed, throughput, and cost. The issues of obsolescence, compatibility, and adherence to accepted standards must be considered in both acquisition and design. Consequently, these important criteria should be an integral part of a comprehensive evaluation methodology.

New research programs are emphasizing the design and development of more powerful supercomputers and of techniques for their utilization. An inability to assess and measure accurately the performance of new architectural designs, which often use many processors in parallel, would inhibit effective development and invite the possibility of overlooking fruitful ideas in architecture and algorithm design. In a real sense, research in new computer architectural concepts drives the need for performance evaluation soundly based in theory.

In recognition of this problem, this committee was to review the state of the art in supercomputer performance evaluation, to identify reasonable expectations for improvement, and to sketch an agenda for research that would lead to the desired improvements. This report is an initial step, which should be followed by support of research by the funding agencies, conduct of research by the academic and industrial communities, and consolidation of progress by a group of qualified experts organized under some formal mechanism.

The remainder of this summary is organized around the conclusions and recommendations of the report, drawing for support on key points from the several chapters.

CONCLUSIONS

The conclusions of the study are stated below, each one followed by a brief discussion.

Conclusion One

<u>Some of the methods, and corresponding metrics, used in the past are not well suited for the performance evaluation of current and future supercomputer systems</u>.

The questions central to the evaluation of supercomputer performance are different in nature from those addressed by the established methods of computer performance analysis; for this reason established methods have not been successfully applied. For example, many current performance models for supercomputers emphasize processor speed in terms of hardware features (instructions, floating point operations, logical inferences, and so forth), ignoring the performance of the other components of the system, such as the operating system, compilers, and input-output devices. Supercomputers have complex structures that make it hard to apply these simple performance models. Today it is axiomatic that supercomputer system performance is a function of problems, implementation, and algorithms. The recent advent of diverse architectures, radically different from each other and from the sequential von Neumann type, has further invalidated a simple approach and made it even more evident that there is an urgent need for the development of methods, models, and metrics capable of describing the performance of the overall system, both hardware and software. The great variety of supercomputer structures in use or being proposed today has precluded even a satisfactory taxonomy of systems, let alone an accurate performance model.

Conclusion Two

<u>Some performance measures and metrics in current use for the evaluation of supercomputers, such as rates of hardware operation and simple kernel execution, are often misleading and misused</u>.

The lack of good methods of performance evaluation for supercomputers has led to extensive use of certain specific measures and benchmarks as indicators of a system's performance. These can be helpful, but they are hard to extrapolate accurately across a variety of machines and algorithms. Several popular metrics (such as peak MFLOPS) and benchmarks exist today; the performance of machines is often quoted in terms of these. The existence of these metrics and benchmarks must be regarded favorably, but their use raises serious questions of oversimplification. They are not meaningful for a wide range of circumstances and applications, and they do not represent the complex relationships between the diverse hardware and software components of a supercomputer. Often, metrics that measure merely hardware features are poorly correlated with the performance of an entire system on a real application. There is, at this time, no agreed upon methodology for the use of benchmarks or their interpretation. There is considerable mistrust of simplistic performance claims throughout the entire supercomputer community.

Conclusion Three

<u>No well developed scientific foundation exists for supercomputer performance evaluation</u>.

Performance evaluation of supercomputers, especially those with parallel architecture, has lagged behind other developments in computer science and engineering. A scientific approach, embracing the diversity and complexity of the systems and providing a clear methodology for evaluating them, would offer better promise of success. A central issue in understanding performance measurements on supercomputers involves the pairing of architectures and applications. Recent work on the study of architectural and algorithmic taxonomies has identified differences that are critical to performance; further work could lead to the successful development of useful and scientific performance models and more systematic, comprehensive benchmarks.

The body of the report outlines a five-stage approach to performance evaluation models: (1) determine the major supercomputer application areas and the predominant mathematical solution techniques, (2) select a collection of representative programs covering scientific disciplines and solution techniques, (3) define the appropriate parameters of the applications and the architectures that will allow models to be developed, (4) define the metrics necessary to understand the performance of the models relative to those parameters, and (5) assess the relationship between the computational and architectural models.

The research agenda in the body of the report, outlined later in our recommendations, should establish the scientific basis that is now insufficiently developed for comprehensive evaluation methods.

Conclusion Four

<u>Performance evaluation of supercomputers is an emerging area of significant interest and importance. There are numerous ongoing efforts by industrial, governmental, and academic laboratories; but more effective mechanisms for teaching, assessing, and disseminating progress in this area are desirable</u>.

There is considerable activity by both vendors and buyers in supercomputer system performance definition. There is increasing research at academic, industrial, and national laboratories supported by significant initiatives by the U.S. Department of Energy; the National Science Foundation; and the U.S. Department of Defense, including the Office of Naval Research and the Defense Advanced Research Projects Agency. These activities reflect the increased importance, and need for progress, in supercomputer performance evaluation. There do not seem to be highly effective mechanisms for the discussion and dissemination of research and of its transfer into methodology. In particular, the committee sees no effective organization to evaluate, track, and translate as rapidly as possible research and experience in this area into commonly accepted criteria for performance evaluation.

RECOMMENDATIONS

On the basis of the foregoing conclusions, the committee offers the following recommendations, each one stated first and then briefly discussed.

Recommendation One

<u>Performance evaluation methods for supercomputer performance, beyond those already available, should be developed and used; and these methods should be based on sufficiently general and unifying concepts to address the whole computer system, including multiple processors, memory, input-output subsystems, and software.</u>

The current unsatisfactory situation in supercomputer performance evaluation can be overcome because better performance models and more systematic and comprehensive test programs are possible. The body of this report outlines a reasonable approach to this end, which should result in methods and measures having validity and usefulness comparable to those currently in use by the general purpose computer performance evaluation community.

The performance evaluation process is cyclic in nature, requiring several iterations for a satisfactory result. We begin with the systems of interest, either existing or proposed supercomputers, and generate either empirical or analytical models of them. We experiment by measuring performance, if the system is an existing computer, or by simulating performance, if the system is a proposed one. The data from the experiments are then combined to give several metrics of performance. The system or the model of it, is modified and the cycle is repeated.

Recommendation Two

<u>Supercomputer systems should be provided with hardware and software for the collection of performance evaluation data</u>.

Some systems come equipped by the vendor with sophisticated hardware and software for collecting performance data. This feature gives the researcher and user the tools for experimentation and observation that are essential to scientific understanding of the key issues underlying performance evaluation.

Recommendation Three

<u>Funding agencies should support more emphasis on supercomputer performance evaluation methods in existing research and development programs, and should initate the support of basic research in the science of supercomputer performance evaluation</u>.

The body of the report suggests an agenda, or framework, for research, the outcome of which is expected to provide the scientific underpinning for a sound methodology of computer performance evaluation. The research framework centers on the following topics:

1. Hierarchical characterization of applications and algorithms in terms of their fundamental units of computation at several levels of resolution.
2. Procedures for synthesizing fundamental arithmetic and logical operations on arrangements of data into powerful computational procedures (algorithms).
3. Procedures for synthesizing fundamental machine functions into application-specific architectures that meet specific performance goals.
4. Methods for modeling and evaluating the performance of supercomputers.

Recommendation Four

<u>The U.S. Department of Energy and the National Science Foundation should undertake a leadership role in establishing a formal mechanism to track, assess, and disseminate research results with a view to bringing about commonly accepted methodologies of supercomputer performance evaluation</u>.

A number of centers supported by the Defense Advanced Research Projects Agency and the Office of Naval Research are actively evaluating novel architectures. The National Bureau of Standards, with support from the Defense Advanced Research Projects Agency, has initiated a research program on the evaluation of performance of diverse architectures. The National Aeronautics and Space Administration both conducts and supports much computer research. The U.S. Department of Energy supports significant research in supercomputer performance evaluation, both in its own laboratories and at universities. The National Science Foundation provides research support in this area to the academic community, and its Directorate for Computer and Information Science and Engineering has a direct interest in supercomputing. Major U.S. vendors have active research and development groups in supercomputer evaluation methods.

The manifold activities taking place in this area would benefit by increased communication and leveraging of effort. Although the development of standards is certainly not appropriate now, the development and distribution of a coherent set of measurement criteria is.

The committee believes it would be desirable for one or two of the federal funding agencies, perhaps in cooperation with others, to establish a group of experts who would, over a period of time, collect and evaluate research results and experience in the area of supercomputer performance evaluation and attempt to translate it into a broadly usable collection of methods and measures. The experience in this field of the U.S. Department of Energy and the recent emphasis on supercomputing at the National Science Foundation suggest that these are the appropriate lead agencies for this task.

INTRODUCTION

Supercomputers allow the solution of computational problems and the simulation of physical phenomena that may not be possible or economic by any other means. However, supercomputers are expensive to acquire and operate, and their design is undergoing rapid and fundamental change. Both of these circumstances demand reliable evaluation of supercomputer performance--on the one hand, to make the most of costly resources and, on the other, to devise and select even more powerful designs.

THE PROBLEM

The task undertaken here is to survey briefly the current state of affairs in the evaluation of supercomputers, to suggest what improvements might be attainable, and to point broadly to desirable directions of inquiry (Appendix A). The problem underlying this task has to do with supercomputers as a unique and costly resource, limitations on available methods of evaluating existing machines, and difficulties in evaluating radically new multiple- and parallel-processor architectures.

A supercomputer is an instance of the most highly performing computer available at a given time. The concept is a dynamic one, changing as advances in computer science and technology are made. As such, the supercomputer is a unique, expensive, and scarce resource, whose full and efficient use is clearly desired.

Methods for evaluating the performance of supercomputers are essential for the proper acquisition and use of computational resources. Appropriate comparisons of performance also allow the proper match of systems to specific applications, leading to optimization of the allocation of computational and economic resources. Moreover, the design of novel models of supercomputers is based on the performance experience of currently available systems and on expectations of future applications. Thus, performance evaluation methodology and performance measures can play an effective role in the exploitation of computational resources and can make the development of new and novel machine designs more cost effective.

A substantial, well organized community of experts exists who specialize in many aspects of performance evaluation: analysis, simulation, monitoring, capacity planning, and measurement. Their successes include analytic models, empirical relations between hardware burst rates and actual computational rates, queuing network models, and prediction of throughput and response time. Nevertheless, it is not possible to say that the fully satisfactory characterization of even sequential, single-processor machines and their workloads is well in hand. The situation with respect to parallel-processor machines and parallel computation models has just begun to be pursued.

The problems we are addressing are fundamentally different from the questions addressed by the expert community just mentioned. The questions here have to do with the measurement of the achievable speed of computation on today's and tomorrow's complex systems, rather than throughput and queuing delays. While it is true that we care about total system performance, it is not so true that we are concerned with maximizing the utilization of each and every system component. Rather, we care that when an application demands a resource, such as an input-output device, that device is available and does not impede the potential performance of the system. Essentially we are most concerned with the computational speed of the processor(s), and we have a secondary interest in the other system components to the extent that they have an influence on the performance of the processor(s).

While it will be possible to use analytic models to understand the performance of supercomputer systems in the future, the technology does not appear to be available now to apply these methods directly, or with any confidence, to supercomputer systems. The basic parameters that must be understood as input to analytic models have not been defined. Where, on conventional sequential uniprocessors, it was possible to estimate, within a reasonable confidence range, the speed of the central processing unit as one resource of a system, today's systems are so application dependent that the range is measurable only in orders of magnitude, not tens of percent.

Moreover, there is a fundamental difference between knowing that an application computes on a system for a certain length of time and knowing that that time is well used. It is this distinction that we propose should be measured and understood. Within a class of the workload, there could be some applications that compute results 10 times faster than other applications. If so, it may be that some of these applications would be more suited to a different architecture or that they should be rewritten to exploit more fully the architecture on which they are executing. Without understanding performance within the processor architecture as something more than an input variable to a global network model, this type of subtlety will not be observed and repaired.

Accordingly, the problem contains such questions as: What methods might be used to evaluate the match between an architecture and an application, given that some variation in both is possible? What measures of performance should be used? How should ease of programming and usability of the system be assessed? What experiments allow the comparing of results?

APPROACH TO THE STUDY

The task of the committee was limited by its charge to a brief, preliminary effort. The central purpose was to identify problems and opportunities and to recommend directions for further action but not to undertake these. The results of this task, accomplished in a few months, are presented in this report. Given its task and the status of the field, the committee did not consider it fruitful to undertake an exhaustive review of the broad area of computer performance evaluation; rather, on the basis of the expertise of its own members and of appropriate contacts within the industrial, research, and user communities, the committee undertook to draw broad conclusions, to sketch improvements that seem attainable in performance evaluation, and to outline an agenda, or framework, for research whose results would underpin the development of an appropriate performance evaluation methodology.

The committee examined the current state-of-the-art methods and practices in the evaluation of supercomputer performance, considering the complexities created by a diversity of available architectures and scientific problem areas. It concluded that the classical measures of performance (millions of instructions per second, millions of operations per second, and millions of floating point operations per second) are simplistic and often misleading. The reason is that supercomputer performance is too complex to be fully characterized by a single figure of merit. The committee also concluded that many of the well developed methods of computer system performance evaluation, and their scientific base, are not appropriate for supercomputers. In short, we lack a complete theory that tells us what the right set of properties should be.

This conclusion led the committee to recommend the development of methods for the evaluation of supercomputer performance applicable to the existence of a variety of architectures and applications. Accordingly, Chapter 2 briefly outlines basic principles, including performance measurement, on which the evaluation of supercomputers ought to be based. Chapter 3 then critiques the current measurement practices on the basis of these principles. Next, Chapter 4 describes some improvements that seem attainable in supercomputer performance evaluation. Finally, Chapter 5 outlines an agenda for research for the development of the scientific base and the measures appropriate for sophisticated evaluation.

PRINCIPLES FOR THE EVALUATION OF SUPERCOMPUTERS

An evaluation of supercomputers may be undertaken for any of several purposes: to choose the machine that best satisfies stated requirements, to allocate machine resources efficiently among many users, to estimate the capability of solving a given problem within constraints of time and cost, or to evaluate alternatives for the design of new supercomputer systems.

THE CONTEXT FOR EVALUATION

As suggested by the definition of the word "evaluate," the purpose of computer evaluation is to determine the value of a computer (and, by implication, the computer system of which it is a major part). However, no evaluation method can determine the value of a computer in the abstract; it is a fundamental principle of computer evaluation that <u>the value of a computer is dependent on the context in which it is used</u>.

The connotation of "context" can be understood through three corollaries of this principle:

Corollary 1: The value of a computer is application dependent.
Corollary 2: The value of a computer is site dependent.
Corollary 3: The value of a computer is time dependent.

Different applications having comparable computational complexity perform differently on the same computer, sometimes by an order of magnitude or more, so the validity of an evaluation is limited to the applications studied. Further, because different computer center sites with similar hardware and software have different application mixes, the validity of an evaluation of a computer for one site or installation may not, and usually does not, extend to others. Finally, applications are continually being refined through changes in programming, algorithms, mathematical methods, and the scientific or engineering principles that are used, so the validity of an evaluation may degrade over time.

In summary, the value of a computer is a dynamic characteristic that is dependent on the changing requirements of the users.

CRITERIA FOR EVALUATION

Figure 2-1 shows a relevance tree for some of the criteria that affect the value of a computer. Qualitative and quantitative criteria are distinguished and discussed briefly below to emphasize that evaluation rests on many factors. One of these factors--performance--is then singled out as the main topic of the report.

Qualitative Criteria

Obsolescence

The value of a computer is in part dependent on its position in its life cycle. If only quantitative measures such as performance and cost are considered in the evaluation, a system can appear to have high value even though it is obsolescent; however, the system may have a relatively short remaining life so the cost per productive year may actually be quite high. Obsolescence is an issue not only for the acquisition of computers but also for their design. For example, the main-memory capacity of supercomputers has increased dramatically in recent years because of the precipitous decline in the cost of random-access memory chips. Thus, to design a supercomputer without a very large real-address space would be an instance of obsolescent design.

Compatibility

A policy in wide use among users of large-scale computers is that a system incompatible with the systems already installed must provide a performance gain commensurate with the cost of conversion. Compatibility is an issue not only in acquisition of existing systems but in the design of new systems: departing from the details of a previous design will often permit higher performance to be achieved but at the cost of conversion efforts by the users.

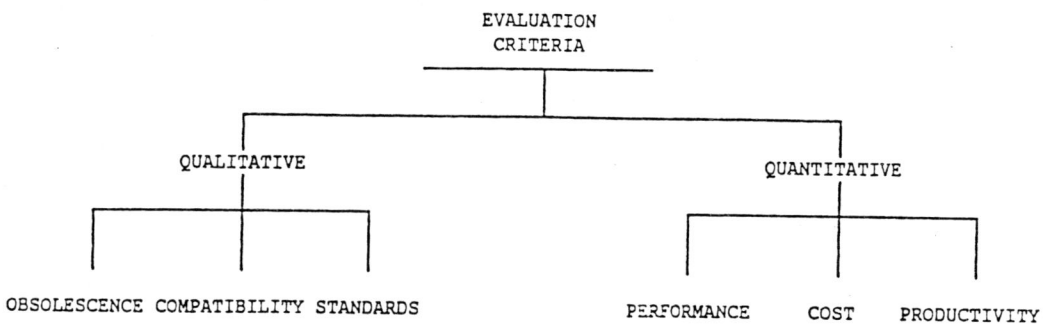

FIGURE 2-1 A relevance tree for supercomputer evaluation.

Standards

Various standards of performance and usage are necessary to computer operations. These standards may pertain to hardware characteristics, interfaces, operating systems, languages, and protocols for communication. Conformity with two kinds of standards, official and de facto, affects the value of supercomputers. De facto standards connote those products that are in use by such a large percentage of a user community that they take on the character of a standard without official promulgation. Examples of de facto standards occur in the minicomputer, main frame, and supercomputer markets, wherever a given product series enjoys a major market share. Operating systems, such as UNIX* and VMS, and languages, such as FORTRAN and ADA, have become de facto standards. Conformity with de facto standards increases the value of a computer because of the large set of user-generated applications and system software available to it and the ease of collaboration with a large set of users. In addition, both kinds of standards facilitate the portability to new machines of operating systems, applications packages, and large programs.

Quantitative Criteria

Performance

Performance evaluation is usually conducted by analytical modeling, simulation, and measurement of the running time of selected codes (commonly called "benchmarking"). Performance criteria for highly complex problems include problem solution time and execution rate; the criterion for large volumes of problems each having low complexity is throughput, that is, the number of problems that can be solved in a given time. In either instance, it is the requirements of the users that determine the appropriate criteria.

Costs

A complete list of costs begins with hardware, software, personnel, operations, and system maintenance. It goes on to include such things

---

*UNIX is a trademark of AT&T Information Systems.

as development of application programs, networking, training, consulting, obsolescence, upgrading, conversion of programs, and documentation. Costs are often underestimated by including only those of acquisition and installation.

Productivity

Productivity is defined as output divided by input, where output includes all results perceived useful by users and input includes all costs to produce the output. Productivity is not adequately measured by the performance and cost of the system alone: the performance and cost of the users themselves must be evaluated. For example, the U.S. Department of Energy high-energy physics community considers "quality of life" to be of equal merit with system performance in assessing the value of a system. Quality of life includes such things as fast response time in an interactive environment, powerful debugging aids, high-speed and easy to use graphics, powerful languages, and optimizing compilers.

MATCHING COMPUTATIONAL AND APPLICATION CHARACTERISTICS

The task of evaluation of supercomputers is conceptually one of matching the characteristics of the computational environment with those of the intended applications. Table 2-1 characterizes various computing resources according to the technologies used in computing environments (processing, storage, input-output, and communications) and the mode of access to those technologies (centralized, distributed, and personal). Centralized resources are those that are shared by a large number of users, typically hundreds to thousands. Distributed resources are usually shared by a tens to hundreds of users, although in principle they are accessible by all users on the network. Personal resources are typically not shared at all. It is the whole environment, not just centralized processing, that must be evaluated in matching resources to requirements.
  In the chapters that follow, the emphasis is on quantitative evaluation of system performance of centralized resources.

THE CYCLE OF PERFORMANCE EVALUATION

Another principle of supercomputer evaluation is that the performance evaluation process is typically cyclic in nature, that is, it may require several iterations through the process before a satisfactory

Table 2-1 Computing Resources by Technologies and Operating Environments

Technologies	Operating Environments		
	Centralized	Distributed	Personal
Processing	Large-scale computers	Mini computers	Micro and personal computers
Storage system	Common file systems	Local disk	Floppy and hard disks
Input-output	High-speed graphics	Medium-speed printers and plotters	Terminals, work stations, and slow printers
Communications	Site networks, LANs [a], and WANs [b]	Site networks, LANs, and WANs	Site networks, LANs, and WANs

[a] LAN = Local-area network
[b] WAN = Wide-area network

result is obtained. Figure 2-2 illustrates the major steps in the cycle. We begin with the systems of interest, either existing or proposed supercomputers, and generate either empirical or analytical models of them. In the past these models have been largely empirical, consisting of relationships drawn from experience in the category of "rules of thumb." For example, a simple empirical rule for estimating scalar performance in floating-point operations per unit time is $1/(12*t_c)$, where t_c is the scalar cycle time. This rule has been found to provide an estimate typically accurate within a few tens of percent. However, the rule does not rest on a theory to explain why it is correct or how to improve on it. To move performance evaluation toward a science it is necessary to go beyond rules of thumb to analytical models that have both explanatory and predictive power, and better accuracy, through the identification of explanatory variables and their relationships. The type of experiments used in this cycle depends on whether the system of interest is an existing computer, in which case its performance can be measured, or whether it is a proposed computer, in which case its performance must be simulated. The raw data obtained from experiments can be combined to give several metrics of performance. These metrics include time metrics such as problem solution time and interactive response time; rate metrics such as millions of instructions per second, millions of floating-point operations per second, and throughput; and cost metrics such as the product of the number of processors and the solution time for parallel processors. Depending on the observed performance, the system may be modified and the cycle repeated.

Evaluation usually requires many iterations of this cycle to satisfy optimization criteria for either selection or design of a supercomputer system. This iterative process is discussed further in Chapter 4.

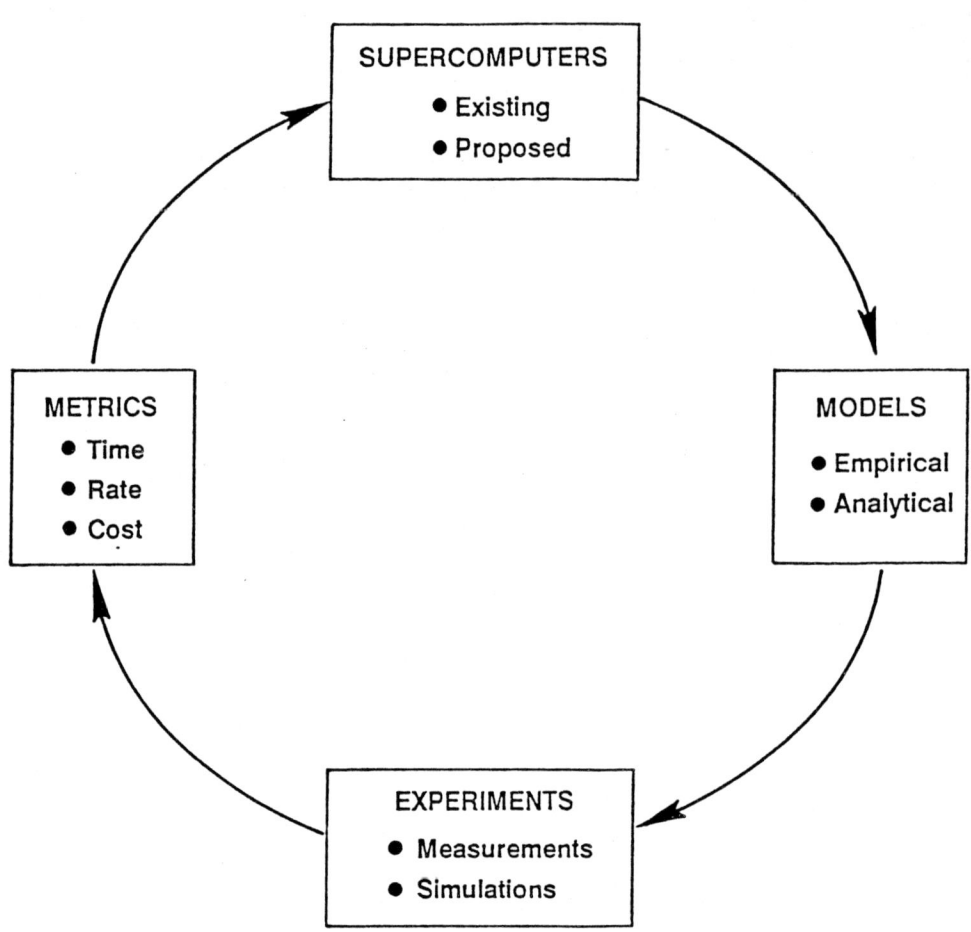

FIGURE 2-2 The cycle of performance evaluation.

THE CURRENT STATE OF THE ART IN EVALUATION OF SUPERCOMPUTERS

Large-scale computations may be characterized as those that require a major fraction of the resources of the most powerful computing systems available at any particular time. Historically, large-scale computations have occurred primarily in areas such as weather forecasting, aeronautical design, orbital mechanics, nuclear energy studies, and nuclear weapon design. Additional areas include automotive design, seismic analysis, petroleum reservoir modeling, condensed matter and statistical physics, nuclear and elementary particle physics, and the modeling of large molecules. Many other applications will emerge in the near future. In many of these areas, scientists and engineers continually face problems whose computational requirements exceed the capability of any available computing system. This is why organizations such as the U.S. Department of Energy (DOE), the National Aeronautics and Space Administration (NASA), and now the National Science Foundation (NSF) have consistently procured and will continue to procure advanced supercomputers as soon as they become available--to treat problems that were previously intractable. These advances challenge existing methods of performance measurement because we cannot precisely forecast the nature of all the computational techniques that eventually will be used in these new applications. Nevertheless, performance measurement of existing systems and workloads provides valuable insight in improving current applications and guiding future developments.

LESSONS FROM THE PAST

The events of the past ten years provide valuable lessons in evaluating performance of large-scale computers. In the early to mid 1970s, machines were introduced with architectures different enough from earlier machines that measurement of their performance was not a simple extension of previous techniques. Before that time, improvements in computer performance came largely through advanced technology and modest architecture improvements, like overlapped operations, which did not impact seriously the algorithms used or the way codes were structured. Noteworthy successes in performance evaluation of sequential instruction machines were achieved and a substantial body of literature on the subject was built.

In the mid to late 1970s the introduction of the ILLIAC IV, STAR-100, Cray-1, and CYBER 2XX series brought the so-called single-instruction multiple-data (SIMD) or "vector" architectures to scientific computing. Access to the potentially high performance of these machines required the codes to be structured to take advantage of machine architectures. In some cases, codes not so structured actually ran more slowly than on previous machines.

While it was relatively easy to estimate or measure the maximum number of floating point operations per second of which SIMD machines were capable, performance of real jobs was much more complicated to assess. Even though most codes were written in FORTRAN language at the time, the ability of the compilers to optimize performance was negligible in the early days. Codes that ran at high performance were painstakingly modified by hand.

During the ensuing ten years, the science of vector computing has come remarkably far. Compiler technology has developed to the point where many constraints are automatically vectorized. Researchers have discovered techniques and algorithms that are well suited to vector machines, including many problems previously thought intractable with these architectures. Today it is axiomatic that supercomputer system performance is a function of problems, implementation, and algorithms. The current trend toward performance enhancement by using multiple processors (multiple vector processors for large applications) brings back all the problems and uncertainties of the early days of vector processing. As with the early days of vector architectures, limited ability exists for the software to partition tasks automatically. Currently, for systems with few (four to eight) processors, partitioning can be done by hand for certain problems; but eventually software will have to improve and there is reasonable expectation that it will. In addition, whereas there is a limited range of variations in SIMD architecture, such as vector length, bandwidth of the communication channels to memory, and start-up time, there are myriad possible multiple-instruction multiple-data (MIMD) architectures. Examples of variations are speed of interprocessor communication and shared versus local memory.

The following conclusion captures these lessons from the past:

Some of the methods, and corresponding metrics, used in the past are not well suited for the performance evaluation of current and future supercomputer systems.

PERFORMANCE METRICS

There are no universally accepted metrics of supercomputer performance. The most widely used metric is millions of floating point operations per second (MFLOPS), or megaflops, which is a partial measure of processor performance. For examples, see Lubeck et al. (1985), Dongarra and Hinds (1985), Los Alamos National Laboratory (in press), and Moore and Bucher (1981). Evaluations based on this metric require great restraint. A cursory examination of the literature reveals that megaflops has been reported to characterize performance with respect to the following diverse features:

- o Peak capability of the hardware
- o Small computational loops
- o Computational kernels extracted from large computations
- o Entire programs
- o Entire workloads.

These measurements can vary widely for the same supercomputer, especially as a function of software and implementation (Worlton, 1984; Dongarra, 1986). So it is always important to know the context in which the measurements are made. Regrettably, such measurements are occasionally lumped together and out of context, particularly in advertising literature. The result is that megaflops, as currently being used, is neither a reliable nor a precise measure of system performance. In spite of these deficiencies, the trade press, having few alternatives, tends to focus on peak hardware rates, so that the problem perseveres.

Also, the floating point operation rate constitutes only a simplistic metric because of certain technical shortcomings:

- o It may not dominate performance for a particular application.
- o It can be hard to measure on real problems.
- o It can be counted in different ways.
- o It can be performed in either scalar or vector mode.

As to the last point, most state-of-the-art supercomputers offer scalar and vector processing. The performance levels of these two modes, as measured in megaflops, may differ by a factor of 5 to 100. Thus, overall performance of an application will depend on the distribution of work between these two modes. This distribution, in turn, depends on the algorithms used, the details of their implementation, and the specific problem being solved.

There is an acute need to develop and use more comprehensive performance metrics than megaflops alone. Some progress has been made. Hockney and Jesshope (1981) have introduced a two-parameter characterization of vector processors. The two parameters are (1) peak, or asymptotic, performance, commonly designated as r_∞, and (2) half-performance vector length, commonly designated as $n_{1/2}$, which is necessary to achieve half the asymptotic performance. This characterization facilitates comparison of different vector architectures as well as assessment of potential performance of a vector processor (Buzbee, in press). A three-parameter model of multiple vector processors is developed in Bucher and Simmons (1985). More work is needed on performance characterizations. In the meantime the following conclusion can be drawn:

<u>Some performance measures and metrics in current use for the evaluation of supercomputers, such as rates of hardware operation and simple kernel execution, are often misleading and misused</u>.

TEST PROGRAMS FOR PERFORMANCE MEASUREMENT

The selection of representative test programs for measurement of the performance range on a supercomputer system is a nontrivial task (Adams et al., 1985). One approach that is growing in acceptance is to define a hierarchy of programs ranging from hardware demonstration programs to full application packages. However, if these application packages are written in FORTRAN language, a barrier to performance evaluation may result because of the major hurdles that FORTRAN puts in the way of algorithmic modification. There is a clear need to start building major benchmark programs that can easily be transported, with appropriate algorithmic changes, to new systems. If performance measurement is to become a science, then the writing of benchmark programs should also be rationalized and not be dependent on ad hoc procedures to overcome the difficulty of FORTRAN for portability.

Hardware Demonstration Programs

Hardware demonstration programs test the basic speed of a machine on simple computational or input-output (I/O) operations. The intent is to have operations that can be measured with no loss of information, yet are simple enough to be analyzed completely. Examples of such operations can be found in Lubeck et al. (1985) and McMahon et al. (1972). From measurements of the basic machine performance, it is possible to determine the costs of memory references, bank conflicts, paging, disk accesses, filling and emptying pipelines, and hitting or missing cache. From this class of programs, it is also possible to determine the vector lengths at which half the peak performance is attained, the vector lengths at which the breakeven point for vector-scalar tradeoffs is reached, the asymptotic peak performance for vector operations, and the amount of work that must be performed between synchronization points in order to overcome the cost of communication in a multiprocessor system.

However, the use of hardware demonstration programs for benchmarking and performance measurement is useful only at a very low level--for machine designers and for providing parameters for use in higher level performance modeling. Results from this level of measurement may not be well representative of supercomputer performance.

Program Kernels

Program kernels represent the computationally intense loops of actual programs; performance on such loops therefore begins to reflect what can be expected of a system when it executes a full workload. Examples include the well-known Lawrence Livermore Loops, commonly used for benchmarking (McMahon, in press), and NASA Ames Kernels (Bailey and Barton, 1985).

In general, such program kernels measure central processing unit (CPU) performance only, although some may be designed to measure primarily I/O performance. Rarely are they designed to measure an integrated system, and their lack of program complexity can create some performance misconceptions. Therefore, relying too heavily on the assumption that there is a high correlation of program kernels with the total workload can pose problems. Finally, because kernels tend to be relatively simple loops in structure, the performance that they individually indicate can vary across the entire range of potential system performance depending on whether the system compiler can recognize vectorizability. If an overall figure of merit must be derived from the sum of such kernels, it should be based on a weighted harmonic mean rather than an arithmetic mean in order to estimate fairly the effects of the peaks and valleys of performance (Worlton, 1984). However, combining a set of measurements into a single number like this should not be done without knowledge of the application environment.

Basic Routines

Basic routines can be defined to represent the main computational elements used in a range of applications. Several examples are given in Table 4-1 of Chapter 4. Another example is LINPACK (Dongarra, 1986). As such, these routines should provide a reasonable indicator of performance for applications in which they consume major portions of the total requisite resources. The performance of a system on these basic routines does not cover the interactions and communications required between them, as well as the remainder of the full application program that is outside their scope. If the time consumed by the remainder of an application is not extremely small relative to the amount of time used by the measured routines, then the value of this set of sample programs declines as a measure of system performance.

Stripped-Down Versions of Major Application Packages

Generally, stripped-down versions of major application packages will retain what we have labeled as basic routines, and they will permit some, but not all, of the interactions required between basic routines. They contain little of the pre- and post-processing required by full application packages and may or may not include interactions of CPU and I/O requirements. A well-known example is the SIMPLE program (Crowley et al., 1978). Stripped-down programs are easier to manipulate and to transport from one system to another than are full application packages, and in cases where the full application packages are proprietary or classified, they permit testing that would otherwise be impossible. One of the problems that often occurs in this type of test routine is that by creating a facsimile of a full program for test purposes, some of the system requirements for memory capacity and I/O performance are relaxed. There is thus a real danger, in constructing a stripped-down version that will fit on a system that must be tested, of losing some of the original structure. In particular, this can create havoc when testing a parallel processing system. For example, if a program is scaled to fit on a system with limited memory, its performance might be totally different from the performance that would be expected if the appropriate memory sizes were maintained. Whereas the version constructed for a large memory might perform well when executed in parallel on a system with sufficient memory, the version constructed for a small memory may appear to spend more time communicating than it would in computing on a balanced system with large memory and fast processors.

Full Application Packages

The class of test programs designated here as "full application packages" provides the most accurate picture of system performance for actual problems, yet it too has drawbacks. Full application packages are hard to transport from system to system because users have adapted them to their own environments, tailoring algorithms to the subtle points of the architecture. Even though the same adaptation will be made in the new environment, it is harder to measure programming style and level of effort invested in fitting a full application package to a given architecture than in doing so for the other types of representative test programs. Measurements on this class of test programs should be made, but are best approached only after the results of measurements on the other test programs have been fully understood and the computing environment has been carefully defined.

Developmental Programs

A final class, developmental programs, reflects the need to consider future workload directions and the need to admit novel approaches to algorithm and architecture design. As such, developmental programs would be used to try out new algorithms, to devise approaches appropriate for new architectures, and to experiment with them. The idea is to be aware of what is just ahead in both algorithm and architecture development, and to plan how to handle new capabilities in software and hardware. In some cases that will mean using radical algorithm approaches to test their utility on existing systems or on new designs. In other cases it will mean staying abreast of new architectures and attempting to design and characterize the programs that will be suitable in this context. Results from developmental programs may be hard to generalize, but should be used to indicate the potential of new supercomputer systems for which new programs would be created and new workloads developed.

ANALYTICAL APPROACH TO PERFORMANCE EVALUATION

The analytical approach to performance evaluation establishes procedures and methods for evaluating performance with respect to some set of applications or computational structures. For examples, see Baskett and Keller (1977) and Bucher and Martin (1982). Benchmarking is often either followed or preceded by modeling to extend the results to other configurations and job mixes. Simulated execution of benchmarks may be used to evaluate systems that are not yet operational. For machines and systems in normal business applications, analytical performance modeling is a mature approach with a strong commercial base.

The literature on analytic performance modeling is extensive, with groups like ACM Sigmetrics, the Computer Measurement Group, and the International Federation of Information Processing Working Group 7.3 on Computer System Modeling devoting annual conferences and publications to the topic. A referreed journal, <u>Performance Measurement</u>, is published quarterly; and the National Science Foundation has sponsored projects in performance evaluation and monitoring for many years. Most of the work is based on the application of queuing theory to computer systems. In spite of the wealth of work, not much has been directly applied to supercomputer systems, primarily because the tradeoffs in supercomputing generally involve maximizing computational performance instead of trying to optimize overall system performance.

SUMMARY

State-of-the-art practice in performance measurement generally involves a hierarchy of test programs wherein each level of the hierarchy has its unique strengths and weaknesses with respect to a specific set of applications or computational structures. Historically, computability has been related primarily to arithmetic complexity, and thus we have naturally evolved toward heavy use of megaflops as a performance metric. However, because of inconsistent practices and some technical shortcomings, this metric should be used with restraint. More work is needed to develop multidimensional characterizations such as those in Hockney and Jesshope (1981).

Perhaps more importantly, we are entering an era in which there will be a diversity of supercomputer architectures, along with a growing set of applications that span a wide spectrum of complexity. Our experience with vector processors demonstrates that as architecture grows in complexity, performance becomes increasingly dependent upon achieving a good match between problems, implementation, and algorithms. This dependence will become even more pronounced as we move into an era of multiprocessor systems. Achieving good matches will hinge to some extent on our capabilities in performance measurement. Thus it will become a much more important aspect of our work, with a corresponding requirement that we nurture advancement of performance measurement technology.

The message of this chapter is crystallized in the following recommendation:

<u>Performance evaluation methods for supercomputers, beyond those already available, should be developed and used; and these methods should be based on sufficiently general and unifying concepts to address the whole computer system, including multiple processors, memory, input-output subsystems, and software.</u>

REFERENCES

Adams, G. B., Brown, R. L. and Denning, P. J. 1985. On Evaluating Parallel Computer Systems. RIACS TR 85.3. Moffett Field, California: Research Institute for Advanced Computer Science. September.

Bailey, D. H., and J. T. Barton. 1985. The NAS Kernel Benchmark Program. NASA Technical Memorandum 86711. Moffett Field, California: Ames Research Center, National Aeronautics and Space Administration. August.

Baskett, F., and T. Keller. 1977. An evaluation of the Cray-1 computer. In High Speed Computer and Algorithm Organization. D. Kuck, D. Lawrie, and A. Sameh, eds. New York: Academic Press.

Bucher, I. Y., and J. L. Martin. 1982. Methodology for Characterizing a Scientific Workload. Unclassified Release LA-UR-82-1702. Los Alamos, New Mexico: Los Alamos National Laboratory.

Bucher, I. Y., and M. L. Simmons. 1985. Performance Assessment of Supercomputers. Computing Surveys. Preprint LA-UR-85-1505. Los Alamos, New Mexico: Los Alamos National Laboratory.

Buzbee, B. L. 1986. A strategy for vectorization. Parallel Computing 3(July):187-192.

Crowley, W. P., C. P. Hendrickson, and T. E. Rudy. 1978. The SIMPLE Code. Report UCID-17715. Livermore, California: Lawrence Livermore National Laboratory. February.

Dongarra, J. J., and A. Hinds. 1985. Comparison of the Cray X-MP-4, Fujitsu VP-200, and Hitachi S-810/20: An Argonne Perspective. Technical Report ANL-85-19. Chicago: Argonne National Laboratory. October.

Dongarra, J. J. 1986. Performance of Various Computers Using Standard Linear Equations Software in a Fortran Environment. Technical Memorandum 23. Chicago: Argonne National Laboratory. April 30.

Hockney, R. W., and C. R. Jesshope. 1981. Parallel Computer Architecture, Programming and Algorithms. Philadelphia: Heydon.

Los Alamos National Laboratory. In press. Los Alamos National Laboratory Computer Benchmarking 1986. LA-10151-MS. Los Alamos, New Mexico: Los Alamos National Laboratory. To be published December 1986.

Lubeck, O., J. Moore, and R. Mendez. 1985. A benchmark comparison of three supercomputers: Fujitsu VP-200, Hitachi S810/20, and Cray X-MP/2. IEEE Computer, 18(12):10-23. December.

McMahon, F. H. In press. The Livermore Fortran Kernels: A CPU Floating Point Performance Range Test. Livermore, California: Lawrence Livermore National Laboratory.

McMahon, F. H., C. J. Sloan, and G. A. Long. 1972. STACKLIB: A Vector Function Library. Report UCID-30083. Livermore, California: Lawrence Livermore National Laboratory. November.

Moore, J. W., and I. Y. Bucher. 1981. Comparative Performance Evaluation of Two Supercomputers: CDC Cyber-205 and CRI Cray-1. Unclassified Release LA-UR-81-1977. Los Alamos, New Mexico: Los Alamos National Laboratory.

Worlton, J. 1984. Understanding supercomputer benchmarks. Datamation, pp. 121-130. September 1.

4

IMPROVEMENTS ATTAINABLE IN PERFORMANCE EVALUATION

> I often say that when you can measure what you are speaking about and express it in numbers, you know something about it; but when you can not measure it, when you can not express it in numbers, your knowledge is of meagre and unsatisfactory kind; it may be the beginning of knowledge, but you have scarcely advanced to the stage of science, whatever that matter may be.
> --Lord Kelvin

Despite the significance of supercomputers to modern science, engineering, and industrial technology, the process of measuring, evaluating, and predicting supercomputer performance is imprecise at best. This chapter describes methods for characterizing applications and architectures and points toward an emerging and promising approach for accomplishing their pairing. It is hoped that this description of what might be attainable will encourage the development of supercomputer performance evaluation as a science.

A central issue in understanding performance measurements on supercomputers involves the pairing of architectures and applications. Is there an inherent matching and, if so, what essential properties of the architectures and applications must be characterized for their contributions to overall system performance? In particular, what attributes enhance the suitability of particular applications for specific architectures? Clear answers to these questions are elusive because the terms "applications" and "architectures" have not been defined precisely. Classifications and formal descriptions are needed to aid in understanding the interaction of hardware and software. That is, only after we have described an application and an architecture within a well defined classification scheme, can we ask what it implies to say that application A has a performance P on machine M. Naturally, experimentation will be a crucial component of the design phase during which these classifications are developed. However, until we are able to define a reference frame around which to develop models of performance, progress cannot be made toward a coherent theory. We may conduct experiments on many discrete applications and architectures without being able to unify and generalize any of the results.

To advance supercomputer performance evaluation as a science, measurements must be made in the context of defined models of architectures and applications. Comparative measurements should be made on a constant set of applications and across a spectrum of systems. As pointed out in Chapter 2, the measurement process should cycle through the construction of abstract theoretical models of applications and architectures, the design of experiments to measure specific parameters relative to those models, the development of metrics and their use in a fully understood environment, and the consequent recreation of basic models.

These observations led the committee to the following conclusion:

<u>No well developed scientific foundation exists for supercomputer performance evaluation</u>.

This is not to say that analytic modeling, mentioned Chapter 3, is not worthwhile or that it is not a well-developed science. It says that it is a science that has been developed to address different issues than the ones in which we are now interested and that, for the performance evaluation questions on which we have chosen to focus, the scientific basis is indeed not present.

MODELS AND CLASSIFICATION SCHEMES

Classifications and formal descriptions may help reduce the continuum of architectures and applications to a reasonable number of cases, and thereby allow their mapping onto manageable sets of information; this may make our matching endeavor more practicable.

Descriptions of Architectures

The taxonomy proposed by Flynn (1972), and introduced in Chapter 3, provides a useful starting point whereby computers can be classified as single-instruction single-data (SISD), single-instruction multiple-data

(SIMD), or multiple-instruction multiple-data (MIMD). Kuck (1978) has transformed this into a considerably more specific classification by distinguishing between <u>multiple or single instruction streams</u> (MIS or SIS) on the one hand, and <u>multiple or single execution streams</u> (MES or SES) on the other. The first distinction is made on the basis of the number of "programs" being executed at once, where a program is assumed to need a single instruction location register in some control unit for its execution. The second distinction is based on the ability of the control unit to sequence one or more operation types at once, where an operation type corresponds roughly to a single operation code. So far the correspondence between Flynn's and Kuck's schemes is obvious.

Going further, Kuck's classification distinguishes between <u>scalar</u> and <u>array</u> (denoted by the addition of the letter A) operation types, where the latter refers to vector instructions of a vector machine like the CYBER 205 as well as to logically corresponding instructions for multiprocessors like the Burroughs BSP.

Thus a CDC 6600 machine can be characterized as SIS-MES, a HEP as MIS-MES, a Cray 1 as SISA-MESA, and an IBM 3090 as SISA-SESA (if one is talking about one processor).

While Kuck's introduction of the instruction and execution layers appears to be convenient and alleviates the ambiguities of Flynn's classification, we feel that we need more ingredients to characterize the performance of a machine and to map an application successfully onto it. The connection scheme between multiprocessors, the memory structure and hierarchy, and the manner in which data items are accessed and manipulated have become meaningful criteria in the description process. Of importance are not only the types of instruction and execution but also categories like the concurrency or complexity of instructions and the source and destination of their operands. Dongarra and Duff (1985) have proposed to describe computers via formalized templates. Other taxonomies have been attempted (for example, Wallich and Zorpette, 1986; Schwartz, 1983) and have highlighted different aspects of architectural characteristics, but each appears to have some weaknesses in addition to its strengths. Although it may not be possible to define a perfect taxonomy of computer architectures that would be free of ambiguity and allow the discrete placement of any system within its structure, much can be learned in the process of seeking definition. Furthermore, for the purposes of performance evaluation, good taxonomy of architectures should permit the development of performance methods and theories for classes of machines, rather than single entities. For these reasons, the continued development of taxonomies should be encouraged.

Descriptions of Applications

Applications can be described at various levels, where the step from one level to the next can be thought of as being one of successive refinement from the general to the specific. The following levels are important ones in this hierarchy:

1. Identification of a scientific or technical problem
2. Choice of mathematical model
3. Choice of "discretization" method (changing from continuous to discrete variables and functions)
4. Identification of "basic" building blocks
5. Choice of numerical methods
6. Arrangement and implementation of algorithms.

The first two levels can be considered as identifying the application. Levels 3 and 4 characterize the "high-level implementation" for reaching the solution. Levels 5 and 6 characterize "intermediate-level" and "low-level" implementation respectively.

It may be useful to note that, although the scientific or technical problem and to a certain extent the mathematical model is given, each of the subsequent steps has an influence on the suitability of the application for a specific architecture. Some of the steps may involve tradeoffs between mathematical properties, like local accuracy or rate of convergence, and more algorithmic aspects, like computational complexity. Having just said this, we must nevertheless admit that massively parallel architectures are having an impact on the development of mathematical models. Research in progress may eventually support arguments for considering only the scientific problem as fixed, and the mathematical model chosen for the solution as being architecture dependent.

When an application is broken down into its main computational elements, it will quite frequently turn out that some of them are of a general purpose type; that is, they occur in many applications from different fields. Let these be called "basic routines," in the sense defined in Chapter 3.

Sameh (1986) has presented a set of applications and a certain number of basic routines contained in them as shown in Table 4-1. Routines that require further partitioning are marked in the table by (*). The basic routines 1 to 10 can be allocated to levels 3 to 5 of the hierarchy mentioned at the beginning of this section. As more applications are added and characterized, the grid should grow much more slowly in the horizontal direction than in the vertical. That is, we expect that a comparatively small set of basic routines, for which the question of an efficient implementation can be thoroughly studied, will

Table 4-1 Basic Routines versus Application Areas

Application Area	Basic Routines[a]									
	1	2	3	4	5	6	7	8	9	10
Computational fluid dynamics	x	x	x	x						
Device simulation	x	x	x					x	x	
Quantum chemistry	x				x					x
Lattice-gauge	x							x		
Structural dynamics	x	x				x				
Circuit simulation	x	x			x	x				
Adjustment of geodetic networks	x						x			
Inverse problems				x			x			
Weather simulation			x	x						
Molecular dynamics					x					

[a] The basic routines are identified as follows:
1. Sparse linear system solvers (*)
2. Nonlinear algebraic system solvers (*)
3. Rapid elliptic problem solvers (*)
4. Fast Fourier transforms
5. Stiff ordinary differential equation solvers
6. Sparse eigenvalue problem solvers (standard and generalized problems)
7. Algorithms for linear least squares, (direct and iterative) (*)
8. Monte Carlo schemes (*)
9. Multigrid schemes (*)
10. Integral transforms

be major constituents of a large spectrum of supercomputer applications.

In addition to giving a functional decomposition of an application, it is useful to present some quantitative information on the computational complexity of its basic routines to understand their relative weights in the total computation. In many cases it will be possible to describe the dimensions of a partial problem in terms of the parameters of the total model. As an illustration one may think of a problem that is based on a K * M * N grid involving the solution of K * M tridiagonal linear systems of dimension N.

In this way we arrive at a formal description of an application, similar in spirit with the one we proposed for the various architectures. Once such a profile is fully constructed, the focus in evaluating the performance of a particular supercomputer system for a given application involves measuring the performance of the basic routines on the computer system and combining the fractional contributions of their occurrence and their respective computational characteristics.

Finally, because alternative approaches to applications may be radically different, new approaches should be included as subcategories of specific application areas as they are developed and studied. For example, computational fluid dynamics has an entry in the Table 4-1 as it stands, but it might have an additional entry that recognizes the characteristics of its solution by methods of cellular automata--a radical and debatable approach--as this technique matures.

Example of an Application

In this section we illustrate the concept of a hierarchical description of an application to indicate that the end user, the scientist who creates applications for supercomputer systems, already views problems in the way that we are advocating. An application refers to a particular implementation of a more general scientific problem. The original problem statement is independent of any notion of machine architecture. As an example, we use the code SNEX as described by Wienke (1985).

The physical problem of interest is in the area of transport physics. The mathematical model chosen to solve this problem involves the solution of the transport equation. The author notes that a choice has been made regarding the solution of the transport equation. Whereas a typical method of solution involves finite difference or finite element techniques on fixed or iteratively defined meshes, this implementation assigns discrete values to some of the independent variables by the discrete ordinates method and then solves the resulting system of uncoupled ordinary linear differential equations. The numerical method chosen to effect the quadratures is an adaptive Newton-Cotes 7-point routine. The SNEX code is the final high-level language encoding of the application for the choices that have been made.

We note that, from the description of SNEX, the hierarchical model that we advocate is not foreign to the developers of large scientific and engineering applications.

REQUIREMENTS FOR PRODUCING MEASUREMENTS

Riganati and Schneck (1984) have observed that there is an absence of basic metrics for calibrating supercomputer performance in an absolute reference frame. As to the parameters noted in Chapter 3 for characterization of vector processors, Hockney (1985) has reported on the utility of $n_{1/2}$, the vector length necessary to achieve half the asymptotic performance; $s_{1/2}$, the parallel task size necessary to achieve half the asymptotic performance; and r_∞, the asymptotic performance in millions of floating point operations per second (MFLOPS). These measures permit the analysis of the overhead associated with the use of vector or parallel hardware features, but they fall short of characterizing the entire system. Additional parameters must be established, and corresponding metrics defined, to permit thorough measurement and comprehensive analysis of the individual components that combine to produce total system performance.

High performance can be achieved only through a combination of hardware and software advances, and these advances must be based on a thorough understanding of the measured interaction of the application and the architecture on which it is executed. Hardware monitors, such as those currently available on the Cray X-MP, provide necessary input to the formulation of models of execution. Software monitors and simulators provide different information and, if designed in a general fashion, can be directed toward understanding performance across systems (Martin et al., 1982; Martin et al., 1983).

Some of the questions that can be resolved by the use of monitoring tools include (but are not limited to) the following:

o   How does the instruction profile of an application change relative to the architecture on which it executes? In particular, how significant to the application are classes of instructions such as floating point operations, integer arithmetic, memory references, jumps, or address computations?

o   For vector architectures how much vectorization is being exploited, how much of the vector power can be used concurrently, what are the average vector lengths, and what are the significant strides?

o   What is the memory referencing pattern? Is it regular? If not, how is it irregular?

o   For a parallel system, what degree of parallelism is being achieved, how much time is wasted when parallel tasks wait to coordinate, and how many memory references are local or global? How much communication is required per computation?

o   How fully is the architecture used? For example, are there instructions, registers, communication links, and other capabilities that are never being used by the compiled code (Summer Workshop on Parallel Algorithms and Architectures, 1986)?

These considerations support the following recommendation:

<u>Supercomputer systems should be provided with hardware and software for the collection of performance evaluation data</u>.

FIVE STAGES IN PERFORMANCE EVALUATION

The following approach attempts to synthesize the considerations described above, outlining several stages in the process of performance evaluation. The goals are both to determine performance capabilities of existing systems and to predict performance of future systems on specified programs, representative of larger classes of applications. Determining the future system requirements for these and developmental applications can provide the means by which to influence designs of future generations of supercomputers.

Stage 1

The first stage in the process is to determine the major supercomputer application areas and the predominant mathematical solution techniques. If radical techniques (for example, chaotic relaxation (Beaudet, 1978)) are under development, they should also be noted. Several reports present some of the current work (Kashiwagi, 1985; Hwang, 1985; Fernbach, 1984; Rodrigue et al., 1984), the report on the Japanese superspeed project being a notable contribution. Evolving areas, such as knowledge processing, should be included, although their characterization will be significantly more difficult.

Stage 2

The second stage is to select a collection of representative programs covering the scientific disciplines and solution techniques for the application areas. For this work, full applications are much more desirable than benchmark programs or simple kernels of problems. Simultaneously, a selection should be made regarding the target architectures for the study. Some effort should be expended at this stage to determine the appropriate representation of the application for the research. Ideally, a machine-independent representation would yield the greatest amount of information, yet this is an unlikely possibility since applications are generally written for a particular architecture. A philosophical choice must be made regarding how extensively to modify a program as it is analyzed on the defined target architectures. Modifications could be high-level language changes to enable execution, syntax changes to permit a compiler to recognize vector and parallel sections of code, algorithmic changes to enhance the suitability of a specific architecture, or total reconsideration of the underlying mathematical model. Clearly, each of these considerations has an associated cost.

Stage 3

The third stage is to define the appropriate parameters of the applications and the architectures that will allow models to be developed. At a practical level, these will be specific architectural and computational models. At a conceptual level, they will provide a frame for abstractions and generalizations. Examples of possible sets of parameters follow.

Architecture Definition, A1

Let the architecture definition, A1, be given by

$$A1 = (N, CT, r_\infty, F, PP, M1, M2, M3, M4, M5),$$

where

o N = number of processors (connection scheme, bandwidth, approximate communication cost, synchronization overhead, $s_{1/2}$)
o CT = cycle time
o r_∞ = peak rate (in MFLOPS)
o F = number of functional units (per processor)
o PP = number of pipes (per processor), cost of use, length
o $M1$ = number of vector registers (per processor), length, $n_{1/2}$
o $M2$ = cache size, access time, cost for misses
o $M3$ = main memory size, access time, contention, banks

- M4 = extended or virtual memory size, access time
- M5 = I/O behavior, bandwidth.

Application Definition, A2

Let the application definition, A2, be given by

$$A2 = (CA, V, P, M, I/O),$$

where

- CA = characteristics of the application (number of floating point operations or logical inferences, amount of memory traffic, total storage requirements, branch behavior)
- V = degree of vectorization (natural and obtainable by a vectorizing compiler), average vector lengths, strides
- P = degree and type of parallelism, granularity, balance
- M = memory references, number relative to floating point operations, access patterns, likelihood of occurring in M1 to M4 as defined above
- I/O = I/O requirements (if they exist beyond the capacity of M4).

Stage 4

In the fourth stage, the metrics necessary to understand the performance of the models relative to the parameters of Stage 3 will be defined. Using these metrics, measurements, for both experimentation and evaluation, can be made in an environment controlled by the investigator. The environment must be defined in a consistent manner, with the realization that changing any of the components of the environment can have an impact on measured performance. Resulting from this stage are an environment vector EV and a performance vector PV.

Environment Vector, EV

Let the environment vector, EV, be given by

$$EV = (A1, C, OS, PE),$$

where

- A1 = architecture definition
- C = compiler (automatic optimization, vectorization, parallelization)
- OS = operating system (scaled toward throughput (multiple users) or turnaround (single user))

o PE = peripheral equipment (for example, I/O system).

Performance Vector, PV

Let the performance vector, PV, be given by

$$PV = (A2, R),$$

where

o A2 = application definition
o R = net processing rate of A1 on A2 (in MFLOPS or millions of operations per second).

Stage 5

Finally, the fifth stage will be to assess the relationship between the computational and architectural models. Is there an inherent pairing? What parameters and metrics are missing? An initial attempt at mapping applications to architectures will be made at this point, and with it an assessment of the performance of specific systems given a predefined applications set. The results will be in the form of a set of ordered pairs of performance information; specifically, each ordered pair will provide the net processing rate of a particular implementation of an application on an architecture, executed within a defined environment. There will not be a single performance value, but rather an array of values. By carefully weighting the elements of the array, classes of applications and architectures will be partitioned according to their mutual conformability.

SYSTEM PERFORMANCE ISSUES

In addition to the challenge of matching applications and architectures, we need technology for specifying and evaluating system performance of advanced architectures. We have noted that the greatest value of increased supercomputer capability lies in the potential to solve problems that are not now solvable, that is, to create new workloads. Thus, not only do we need advanced architectures, we also need productive environments for developing new applications. Designers have always attempted to balance supercomputer systems carefully; for example, high-performance processors were complemented by large memories and large bandwidth I/O. Future supercomputers should present a balanced hardware-software system that includes the following features:

o Efficient management of asynchronous tasks and efficient interprocessor communication
o Large, efficient memories
o High-speed channels and peripherals
o High-performance secondary storage
o High-speed networking technology, for example, protocols and interfaces
o Very high-speed graphics
o Program monitors (profilers)
o Productive environment for software development and management
o Hardware assists for debugging and performance measurement
o Fault tolerance and graceful degradation of multiprocessor systems
o Scalability to various sizes, so that expansion will permit upward compatibility of applications programs, and so that small versions may be built with identical software interfaces.

System measurement and evaluation are extremely complex. Thus, they are active areas of basic research that merit encouragement.

CONCLUSION

The performance of an application on an architecture cannot be considered in isolation. The execution environment, including the compiler, operating system, and peripheral equipment, must be fully understood before measurements can be analyzed in context. Defining and quantifying these contributions and also accounting for the level of human effort required to use a system efficiently are critical to the scientific evaluation of supercomputer performance.

We have presented a method for structuring experiments to measure performance within a controlled environment. By developing detailed descriptions of applications and architectures within this context, and using the information gathered at successive stages of the defined hierarchies, we hope to model the performance of an application on a supercomputer system. Information at the lowest levels will provide the processing potential of each possible computational mode (scalar, vector, parallel), and extensions of Amdahl's Law (Amdahl, 1967) will direct us toward expectations of total performance based on the relative weights assigned to the various processing modes for a given workload.*

---

*Amdahl's Law gives the ratio of the time t_0 to do a given task at a given rate to the time to do do it if the task is divided into a fraction f, performed at the given rate, and a fraction 1 - f, performed at a rate r times as great. The relationship may be written symbolically as $t_0/t = (f + (1 - f)/r)^{-1}$.

This theoretical prediction will then be tested against measurements of the system on the given workload. If the comparison of expected and achieved performance produces large discrepancies, then the models will be re-examined and modified to include information that was initially missing. Successive iterations of this process, as suggested by Figure 2-3, should enable the understanding of current system performance, and should permit reasonable predictions of future behavior of modified workloads on the current system, or of the current workload on a different system. Critical to the entire process is the recording of sufficient information concerning the environment of the experiments to ensure reproducibility.

The goals of this plan are long term. Nevertheless, there is much to be learned incrementally. Requirements for fulfilling the goals, such as tools for making and analyzing measurements, can have an immediate impact on current performance evaluation work. Certainly, architecture designers, application developers, and system engineers will all profit from the establishment of a body of information, collected in a scientific manner, describing the analysis and measurement of a variety of applications on a spectrum of existing computer systems.

This chapter has pointed to research directions that should extend the scope of supercomputer performance evaluation. The level of interest in the field may be inferred by the numerous references cited. Chapter 2 discusses the importance of the topic, while Chapter 5 cites various programs with interest in high-performance computing and associated evaluation of it. As the field advances, increased interaction among its participants will enhance the usual verification and adoption of useful results. The following conclusion embraces these points:

<u>Performance evaluation of supercomputers is an emerging area of significant interest and importance. There are numerous ongoing efforts by industrial, governmental, and academic laboratories; but more effective mechanisms for teaching, assessing, and disseminating progress in this area are desirable</u>.

REFERENCES

Amdahl, G. 1967. The validity of the single processor approach to achieving large scale computing capabilities. American Federation of Information Processing Societies Conference Proceedings. Vol. 30.

Beaudet, C. M. 1978. Asynchronous iterative methods for multi-processor. Journal of the Association of Computing Machinery. Vol. 25. April.

Dongarra, J. J., and I. S. Duff. 1985. Advanced Architecture Computers. Technical Memorandum 57. Chicago: Argonne National Laboratory. October 10.

Fernbach, S. 1984. Applications of supercomputers in the USA--today and tomorrow. In Supercomputers: Design and Applications. Los Alamitos California: Computer Society, Institute of Electrical and Electronics Engineers.

Flynn, M. J. 1972. IEEE Transactions on Computers C-21:948-960.

Hockney, R. W. 1985. (r_∞, $n_{1/2}$, $s_{1/2}$) Measurements on the 2-CPU Cray X-MP. Parallel Computing 2:1-14.

Hwang, K. 1985. Multiprocessor supercomputers for scientific/engineering applications. IEEE Computer 18(6):57-83.

Kashiwagi, H. 1985. The Japanese super-speed computer project. Future Generations Computer Systems 1:(3)153-160.

Kuck, D. J. 1978. The Structure of Computers and Computations. Vol. 1, pp. 316-318. New York: John Wiley & Sons.

Martin, J. L., I. Y. Bucher, and T. T. Warnock. 1982. Workload Characterization: Tools and Techniques. Technical Report LA-UR-82-3213. Los Alamos, New Mexico: Los Alamos National Laboratory. December.

Martin, J. L., A. L. Dana, and T. T. Warnock. 1983. Tools for measuring software performance of vector architectures. In Proceedings. Symposium on Application and Assessment of Automated Tools for Software Development. November.

Riganati, J. P., and P. B. Schneck. 1984. Supercomputing. IEEE Computer 17(10):97-110.

Rodrigue, G., et al. 1984. Large-scale scientific computation. In Supercomputers: Design and Applications. Los Alamitos, California: Computer Society, Institute of Electrical and Electronics Engineers.

Sameh, A. 1986. Personal communication. Urbana, Illinois: University of Illinois. March.

Schwartz, J. 1983. A Taxonomic Table of Parallel Computers Based on 55 Designs. Technical Report UCN-69. New York: Courant Institute, New York University.

Summer Workshop on Parallel Algorithms and Architectures. 1986. Report. UMIACS-TR-86-1, CS-TR-1625. College Park, Maryland: University of Maryland. February.

Wallich, P., and G. Zorpette, eds. 1986. Minis and mainframes. IEEE Spectrum 23(1):36-39. January.

Wienke, B. R. 1985. SNEX: Semianalytic solution of the one-dimensional discrete ordinates transport equation with diamond differenced angular fluxes. Computer Physics Communications 38:397-402.

5

AN AGENDA FOR RESEARCH

This chapter restates the problem identified in the previous chapters: specifically, the need for research to develop methods for evaluating supercomputer performance. An agenda, or framework, for such research is proposed here. Implementation of this agenda will involve the entire large-scale computing community and should be integrated into existing and developing research programs. This integration will be most successful if progress is monitored and stimulated by a body of representatives of various funding and performing agencies as well as academic, industry, and government experts.

OPPORTUNITIES

The design space for computer systems has been dramatically enlarged by growth in microelectronics and emergence of parallel structuring of computations as a means for increasing the performance of computer systems on specific applications. These trends provide an opportunity to match the computational structure of applications and algorithms with the capabilities of system architectures. Parallelism, which will be a critical factor in attainment of high performance, adds additional degrees of freedom and complexity to both computation structures and architectures. At the same time, system architectures are typically built from operations on data structures, whereas scientific and engineering applications are expressed in terms of equations to be solved or relationships to be resolved. The expression of an application as operations on data structures usually introduces many additional steps to the computation structure. Awkward mappings from applications to system architectures may result in substantially lower performance than the system is capable of. Consequently, we outline areas of research that may provide more efficient and effective methods of accomplishing the following tasks:

- o Mappings of applications onto architecture
- o Synthesis of operations into algorithms
- o Applications-specific architectures
- o Performance modeling.

RESEARCH PROGRAM SPECIFICATIONS

Current design and design evaluation methods skip from gross specification requirements to microscopic design levels. This leads to bottom-up construction of system architectures, which may or may not meet application requirements. Because of the synergy between architecture (design), problem formulation, and implementation, synthesis of computation structures with design methods will be necessary. Thus we propose a hierarchical approach with the following elements. Appendix B gives further examples.

Hierarchical Characterization of Applications and Algorithms

The earliest use of electronic computers entailed decomposition of applications into rather simple fundamental units of computation--for example, arithmetic operations and loops. It was quickly realized that certain "functions" were common to many applications--for example, elementary trignometric functions and input and output of various types of data. Thus, "libraries" of software packages and subroutines quickly emerged and frequently served as "building blocks" for constructing application programs. This trend has continued and today we have large collections of software modules or basic routines in such areas as linear algebra, interpolation, approximation, and sorting, such as listed in Table 4-1. These collections have even begun to reflect the architecture of supercomputers. For example, the LINPACK collection for linear algebra has been formulated hierarchically in terms of basic vector operations. These vector operations are chosen to assure high performance on a wide range of architecture. And in general there is a trend toward formulation of applications in terms of "high-level operators" with the operators being chosen so that they can be implemented efficiently on supercomputers.

Thus we recommend a broad and systematic study to characterize applications and algorithms in terms of "fundamental units of computation." The work by Sameh (1986) identifying basic routines common to many application areas, cited in Chapter 4, is illustrative of what is needed. The applications to be studied should include energy, aerospace, real-time control, sensor data analysis, and intelligent control. Given current trends in microelectronics, if a sufficiently powerful set of high level operators can be identified, then it may be advantageous to incorporate them directly into hardware. And whether they are in hardware or not, use of such a set may significantly simplify and improve mappings of applications onto architectures.

Composing Operations into Algorithms

Research is needed to develop procedures for composing operations on data structures into parameterized algorithm elements. For example, a programmable systolic array with addition and multiplication operations can be used to construct "optimal" computation structures for a spectrum of the algorithms used in vision. In other words, one starts with a set of fundamental units of computation and then explores composition of them into algorithms. A key research issue is whether a somewhat general capability can be established wherein efficient structures can be systematically produced for broad classes of algorithms.

Application-Specific Architectures

Research is needed to develop procedures for synthesis of application-specific architectures that must meet specific performance goals.

There are a number of projects under way to develop application-specific architectures. The image and signal processing communities have been particularly successful in this area. Other activities include projects to build architectures for physics related problems and projects for building architectures for production rule systems and logic programming. The Numerical Aerodynamic Simulation system, sponsored by the National Aeronautics and Space Administration, is a large-scale program for development of a computer facility capable of solving equations governing the fluid dynamic flows about aerospace vehicles, even though it uses general purpose, rather than application-specific, supercomputers. A key research issue is whether procedures can be developed for synthesis of application-specific architectures. The objective is a capability for efficiently developing architectures that meet performance goals for special applications.

Hierarchical Performance Modeling of Supercomputers

Research is needed to advance significantly methods for modeling and evaluating the performance of supercomputers. As noted throughout this report, as architecture grows in complexity, performance becomes increasingly dependent on achieving a good match between problems, implementation, and algorithms. Achieving that match in turn will depend partly on our capabilities in performance measurement. Particularly important will be the development of multidimensional performance models and provision of hardware facilities for collecting associated data. The latter should be encouraged in all experimental equipment. Further, several commercial supercomputers now provide capability for collecting a variety of performance data. Study and dissemination thereof should be nurtured. These topics should also be evident in the curriculum of major universities.

The corollary to the specification of such a research program is a recommendation for its support:

<u>Funding agencies should support more emphasis on supercomputer performance evaluation methods in existing research and development programs, and should initiate the support of basic research in the science of supercomputer performance evaluation.</u>

CONDUCT OF RESEARCH PROGRAM

Although this research program can be established and developed in the context of existing federal government agencies that sponsor research in very high-performance computation, it will be most successful if it is given focus and direction by a group of experts who represent interested funding agencies, other government interests, academicians, and the private sector. Because the research effort will be a natural part of diverse projects that are under the auspices of many agencies, the vision and framework for the development of scientific supercomputer performance evaluation should be consolidated within a group that can serve as advisors to the general community of researchers and funding organizations.

Programs with known active interests in very high-performance computation include the U.S. Department of Energy, the National Aeronautics and Space Administration, several U.S. Department of Defense agencies, including the Defense Advanced Research Projects Agency and the Strategic Defense Initiative Office, as well as some of the basic research agencies, such as the Office of Naval Research and the Air Force Office of Scientific Research. These programs should all have a component of evaluation in their research funding. The new Directorate for Computer and Information Science and Engineering at the National Science Foundation is also a potential sponsor for such a research thrust. The National Bureau of Standards has a research program under way that addresses performance measurement of computers, especially the multiprocessor machines that are the subject of much current development. Possible means of implementing this and similar programs have been sketched in two reports on very high performance computing research prepared respectively by the Federal Council on Science, Engineering, and Technology (Kahn, 1985) and the White House Science Council (Browne, undated). One implementation strategy is to set up coordinated programs in the interested agencies together with a mechanism to insure optimum choice of research directions and close cooperation among programs.

The manifold activities taking place in this area would benefit by increased communication and leveraging of effort. Although the development of standards is certainly not appropriate now, the development and distribution of a coherent set of measurement criteria are.

The committee believes it would be desirable for one or two of the federal funding agencies, perhaps in cooperation with others, to establish a group of experts who would, over a period of time, collect and evaluate research results and experience in the area of supercomputer performance evaluation and attempt to translate it into a broadly usable collection of methods and measures. The experience in this field of the U.S. Department of Enregy and the recent emphasis on supercomputing at the National Science Foundation suggest that these are the appropriate lead agencies for this task.

Thus a final recommendation is intended to translate research and experience into a commonly agreed collection of performance models, methods, and measures for practical use:

The U.S. Department of Energy and the National Science Foundation should undertake a leadership role in establishing a formal mechanism to track, assess, and disseminate research results with a view to bringing about commonly accepted methodologies of supercomputer performance evaluation.

REFERENCES

Browne, J. C., Chairman. Undated. Research in Very High Performance Computing: A Policy Recommendation and a Research Requirements Statement. Submitted by the White House Science Council Committee on Research in Very High Performance Computing. Washington: Office of Science and Technology Policy, Executive Office of the President.

Kahn, R. E., Chairman. 1985. Report of the Federal Coordinating Council on Science, Engineering, and Technology. Panel on Advanced Computer Research in the Federal Government. Washington Office of Science and Technology Policy, Executive Office of the President. June.

APPENDIX A

STATEMENT OF TASK

The task of the committee, as originally conceived, is described in the following excerpt from the Notice of Financial Assistance Award from the U.S. Department of Energy and the Research Grant from the Office of Naval Research to the National Academy of Sciences:

> The committee will carry out Phase I of a study to define criteria for the development and performance measurement of large-scale computers for scientific and engineering applications. Phase I will synthesize a collective judgment on the best study plan for the substantive aspects of the supercomputer criteria question. (Phase II will carry out the substantive study, provided that the plan developed in Phase I appears promising.) The committee will perform the following tasks:
>
> 1. Select important, computationally intensive problems related to large-scale scientific and engineering applications to constitute the subject matter of the study.
>
> 2. Examine the computational characteristics of these problems together with the capabilities of existing and prospective large-scale computers so as to develop a study plan that will assess the prospects of improved criteria for large-scale computer development and performance measurement, the nature of such improvements, and the anticipated consequences of these improvements.
>
> 3. Document the results of Phase I.

The committee will consist of approximately ten recognized experts in the following areas: numerical processing, symbolic processing, algorithm design, computer architecture, computational physics, computational mechanics, and computer performance measurement.

During the course of the study, a different emphasis of the Phase I task was recommended by the committee and accepted by the representatives of the sponsors. In particular, Phase I undertook to describe the problem of performance measurement in some depth and to point broadly to desirable directions of inquiry. However it was believed that the detailed definition of a research program to resolve the problem could be done more productively by the supercomputer community itself than by this, or any other, committee. Consequently no study plan is proposed for Phase II. Instead a different need is seen--a forum to track, assess, and disseminate progress, so that research results get promptly translated into practice.

APPENDIX B

ANNOTATED SHORT BIBLIOGRAPHY OF ALGORITHM- OR
APPLICATION-SPECIALIZED COMPUTER SYSTEMS

This annotated bibliography lists and briefly discusses some literature on computer systems that have been built to execute one or a small number of computation structures with maximum speed. The common characteristic is parallelism. The common design theme is to create a configuration of processors and interconnections that can execute specific parallel computation structures at full capacity of all of the processors. This research has a long history in some application areas and a much briefer history in others. Architectures for efficient high performance execution of low-level vision algorithms have been studied intensively. Intensive attention to other application areas has only recently developed. This bibliography makes no claim for completeness. It is intended to give a representative sample of research.

BOOKS, CONFERENCE PROCEEDINGS, AND JOURNALS

There are several edited books and a number of conference proceedings that collect many examples of algorithms or application-specific architectures. The following items are representative:

Computer Graphics and Image Processing. (This journal includes many articles on specialized architectures for image processing.)

Duff, M. J. B., ed. 1982. Languages and Architectures for Image Processing. New York: Academic Press. (Most of the early major projects for image processing systems are represented in this volume.)

Matsen, F. A., and T. Tajima, eds. 1986. Supercomputers: Algorithms, Architectures and Scientific Computation. Austin,

Texas: University of Texas Press. (The chapters by Hagstrom, Kung, Leventhal et al., Reeves, and Winkler et al., are germane. The articles are mostly written by application discipline scientists.)

Institute of Electrical and Electronics Engineers. 1983. IEEE Computer Society Workshop on Computer Architecture for Pattern Analysis and Image Database Management. Pasadena, Calif. October.

Preston, K., and L. Uhr, eds. 1982. Multi-Computers and Image Processing. New York: Academic Press.

SPIE Symposium on Architecture and Algorithms for Digital Image Processing. 1984. Proceedings. San Diego. August.

Tanimoto, S. L., and A. Klinger, eds. 1980. Computer Vision: Machine Perception Through Hierarchical Computation Structures. New York: Academic Press.

JOURNAL ARTICLES, CONFERENCE PROCEEDING ARTICLES, AND REPORTS

This section gives a selection of articles by topic. Some effort has been made to identify continuing substantive projects.

Linear Algebra Systems

Armano, H., et al. 1985. $(SM)^2$-II: A new version of the sparse matrix solving machine. Pp. 100-107 in Proceedings of the 12th Annual International Symposium on Computer Architecture. June.

Chuang, H. Y. H., and G. He. 1985. A versatile systolic array for matrix computations. Pp. 315-322 in Proceedings of the 12th Annual International Symposium on Computer Architecture. June.

Hoshino, T., et al. 1983. Highly parallel processor array "PAX" for wide scientific application. Pp. 95-105 in Proceedings of the 8th International Conference on Parallel Processing. August.

Computations in Physics

Beetem, J., et al. 1985. The GF11 supercomputer. Pp. 108-113 in Proceedings of the 12th Annual International Symposium on Computer Architecture. June. (The key feature of the GF11 is its configurable network switch, which allows the establishment of a set of algorithm-specific topologies for a single-instruction multiple-data processor array. Its intended application is quantum chromodynamics.)

Christ, N., and A. Terrano. 1984. A very fast parallel processor. IEEE Transactions on Computers C-33:344-350. (Another quantum chromodynamics system.)

Numerical Aerodynamic Simulation

The National Aeronautics and Space Administration (NASA) initiated the Numerical Aerodynamic Simulation (NAS) program in 1983 to design a computational system capable of solving the Navier-Stokes equation to a degree of resolution that would permit the computer to be a major complement to wind tunnels. The report literature on the project can be obtained from NASA's Ames Research Center.

WARP Project

Kung, H. T. 1984. Systolic algorithms for the CMU WARP processor. Pp. 570-577 in Proceedings of the 7th International Conference on Pattern Recognition. June. (The WARP project under the direction of H.T. Kung at Carnegie-Mellon University, is developing a computation engine [WARP] that can execute the computations needed to control an autonomous load vehicle. The algorithm set includes image analysis, differential equations for mechanical control, and artificial intelligence. There is a large literature.)

Symbolic Processing

The three main threads of research in symbolic processing are PROLOG machines, production rule machines, and list processing (LISP) machines. The Japanese Fifth Generation Computer Project stimulated much activity in this application. We give only a slender slice of the recent literature to allow the interested reader to work his way back through references.

Nakagaki, R., et al. 1985. Design of a high-speed prolog machine (HPM). Pp. 191-197 in Proceedings of the 12th Annual International Symposium on Computer Architecture. June.

Stolfo, S., and D. E. Shaw. 1982. DADO: A tree structured machine architecture for production systems. In Proceedings National Conference on Artificial Intelligence.

Speech Recognition

Speech recognition algorithms are different from vision. We give two recent reference.

Anantharaman, J., and R. Bisions. 1986. A hardware accelerator for speech recognition algorithms. In Proceedings of the 13th International Symposium on Computer Architecture. June.

Digital Filters

Lu, H.-H., E. A. Lei, and D. G. Messerschmitt. 1985. Fast recursive filtering with multiple slow processing elements. Proceedings IEEE Transactions on Circuits and Systems 32:1119-1129.

Schwartz, D. A. 1985. Synchronous Multiprocessor Realizations of Shift-Invariant Flow Graphs. Ph.D. Thesis. Atlanta, Georgia: School of Electrical Engineering, Georgia Institute of Technology. June.